Gen Z Dictionary

The A-Z Slang Guide to Decoding, Understanding and Speaking the Gen Z Language with Common Emojis Gestures

Daniel Ford

ISBN-13: 979-8322007234

DEDICATION

To every one of my readers!

TABLE OF CONTENT

Introduction

The group of individuals that is getting the most attention has been dubbed Generation Z, or Zoomers for short, as they are more frequently referred to. Many things set this generation apart from the generations of people who came before them, apart from their lofty goals and colloquial language. However, what does the language of Generation Z mean?

Who is the Gen Z?

While it might appear like a simple question, there is no definitive answer concerning the age gap. Based to the Pew Research Center, everybody born between 1997 and 2012 classifies as Gen Z for their surveys. This provides a very accurate definition; nevertheless, the precise dates could vary slightly in other parts of the world.

Referring back to the research studies carried out by the Pew Research Center, we could notice specific differences between Gen Z and the previous generations. To start with, it is more knowledgeable and diversified compared to any generation before it. Regarding political thought, it also tends to be more liberal when it comes to topics like climate change, racial discrimination, and same-sex marriage. These outcomes are not surprising because they all mirror long-standing patterns, but these political and demographic distinctions are important in Generation Z's language and identity.

Gen Z's Linguistic Code

The words and phrases that are created by a generation of people are perhaps the most distinctive component of the language they use. Considering young people tend to be the most adventurous with language, Zoomers currently have the most recent and diverse vocabulary.

It goes without saying that especially as you grow more mature, the way you speak evolves. And it's even more apparent when you observe other generations of people. Over time, you will grow into and out of cohorts, regardless of which one you are born into, and remain in the same generation for the rest of your life.

Studying cohorts has demonstrated to us that as people grow older and move from adolescence to adulthood, they seem to grow more conservative. Several nouns that end in "-ing" tend to be pronounced by adolescents in America as "-in" terms. Therefore, they use "talkin" rather than "talking." and walkin as opposed to walking.

However, as the kids get older, they start speaking words properly. In simple terms, after joining the workforce, people start using more "conservative" as well as socially acceptable language. Gen Z is presently the least conservative generation. When compared to what their predecessors did in the past, they are far more inclined to experimenting and attempting what they hear other people are doing.

Traits of the Generation Z

- **Diverse**

The vast majority of this generation is considerably more diverse than previous generations have been in regard to race and ethnicity. Also, when compared with generations before them, they have a more accepting and empathetic culture that promotes the inclusion of gender and race.

- **Researchers**

With technology right in their hands, many Zoomers research online feedback, evaluations, and details before committing to a purchase or accepting a deal.

- **Digital Natives**

While discussing technology, it's important to point out that Generation Z barely recognizes an age before phones and the internet. When compared to earlier generations, their generation is significantly more proficient at understanding technology.

- **Impatient**

The current generation tends to be impatience as technology makes everything considerably easier. Their wants are clear, and they seem to have them now. They were brought up in a society where same-day delivery services are the standard as opposed to an additional benefit.

- **Competitive**

Generation Y has become known for its excellent teamwork and cooperation. However, this generation is different. As a result of their strong independence, they are subject to a great deal of competition.

- **Adaptable With regard to Location**

The COVID-19 pandemic demonstrated, if nothing else, how versatile this present generation is regarding location and timing. In order to communicate with another person, they are not always required to be present in the same location. This is an issue for generations before them, and millennials especially find it hard to maintain distant relationships.

Language Glossary

A

- **Af/Asf**

International Phonetic Alphabet: əzˈfək

Meaning: Abbreviated form of "as fuck."

For Example: "The game was lame as fuck." "David is lazy asf!"

- **Asl**

International Phonetic Alphabet: əzˈhɛl

Meaning: Abbreviated form of "as hell."

For Example: "The weather is hot asl."

- **Airtight**

International Phonetic Alphabet: ˈɛrˌtaɪt

Meaning: Something that is thought to be basically flawless and unimprovable.

For Example: "The contract was quite airtight"

- **Ate**

International Phonetic Alphabet: ˈeɪt

Meaning: The colloquial phrase is used to describe someone who is doing well or in a fashionable manner.

For Example: "I noticed your Instagram post. You truly ate in that dress"

- **Aight**

International Phonetic Alphabet: ˌɔlˈɹaɪt

Meaning: A different form of writing alright.

For Example: "Aight, I will go visit her tomorrow."

- **Aesthetic**

International Phonetic Alphabet: ɛsˈθɛtɪk

Meaning: The term "aesthetic" defines the various ways that Gen Z pursues their style and methods of expressing themselves. It could have to do with their interests, general ambiance, music choice, bedroom design, or their sense of fashion.

For Example: E-girl/E-boy, Y2K, Downtown Girl, Dark Academia

- **Amirite**

International Phonetic Alphabet: əm aɪ ˈɹaɪt

Meaning: The shortened version of "Am I Right?"

This expression tends to be used to highlight an argument that the two parties consider agreeable and doesn't necessitate a response.

For Example: "The weekend could not get here sooner, amirite."

B

- **BDE**

International Phonetic Alphabet: ˈbɪg ˈdɪk ˈɛnɚˈdʒi

Meaning: An acronym for "big dick energy." A term that defines a person who seems relaxed and confident.

For Example: "He just has BDE."

- **Bruh/Brov**

International Phonetic Alphabet: ˈbɹəðɚ

Meaning: Abbreviated form of the word "brother"

For Example: "Did you place the order? Bruh!"

- **Bffr**

International Phonetic Alphabet: ˈbi ˈfəkɪŋ ˈɹiəl

Meaning: The acronym for "Be fucking real." That indicates "taking something seriously" or reacting to an incident that appears so unbelievable that it almost seems unbelievable.

For Example: "You really want to wrestle in the WWE? Bffr."

- **Body Count**

International Phonetic Alphabet: ˈbɑdi ˈkaʊnt

Meaning: A secret phrase indicating the number of individuals someone has slept with.

For Example: "I heard she has a body count less than 7."

- **Big Yikes**

International Phonetic Alphabet: ˈbɪg ˈjaɪks

Meaning: When "Yikes" does not adequately express how embarrassed you are, then use this.

For Example: "I can't believe you were caught doing that, big yikes"

- **Boujee**

Meaning: When describing someone or something as being extravagant or fancy, you use this term.

For Example: "I don't like Taylor, he's always to boujee"

- **Bop**

International Phonetic Alphabet: ˈbɑp

Meaning: Whenever an album or song is exceptional.

For Example: "Rihanna's new single is just bop"

- **Bet**

International Phonetic Alphabet: ˈbɛt

Meaning: This simply signifies "yes," "I'm down," or some sort of acceptance of something.

For Example: "Are you coming tonight?" "Bet!"

- **Beat your face**

International Phonetic Alphabet: ˈbit jɚ ˈfeɪs

Meaning: The act of applying beauty products is what is referred to by the term. Typically used by beauty influencers

For Example: "I need to beat my face for today's event"

- **Bae**

International Phonetic Alphabet: ˈbaɪ

Meaning: An affectionate expression for someone you are romantically attached to.

For Example: "I can't wait to see my bae tonight."

- **Basic**

International Phonetic Alphabet: ˈbeɪsɪk

Meaning: Used to refer to an individual who lacks personality or is unoriginal.

For Example: "She's so basic, she always wears the same outfit."

- **Bussin'**

International Phonetic Alphabet: ˈbəsɪŋ

Meaning: What you could say in an instance of something pleasant or good.

For Example: "That party on Saturday was bussin!"

- **Bestie**

Meaning: A best friend is usually referred to as a bestie.

For Example: "Damien is my Bestie"

- **Big Mad**

International Phonetic Alphabet: ˈbɪg ˈmæd

Meaning: This is a different way of communicating your intense anger over something.

For Example: "I am big mad this furniture was not delivered today."

- **Bih**

International Phonetic Alphabet: ˈbɪtʃ

Meaning: While it is sometimes used as an affectionate word amongst friends, a bih represents a derogatory version of bitch.

For Example: "Sussan is such a bih"

- **Bye Felicia**

International Phonetic Alphabet: baɪ fəˈlɪʃə

Meaning: Whenever you bid farewell to something or someone who is departing although aren't particularly concerned that they are going, you use the expression "bye Felicia."

For Example: When referring to the exit of an horrible boss, you could say, "Bye Felicia!"

C

- **Cap**

International Phonetic Alphabet: ˈkæp

Meaning: Cap indicates lying. Saying "no cap" indicates your honesty. You are telling the truth or being real.

For Example: "I call cap on everything Dave said"

- **CEO**

International Phonetic Alphabet: ˌsiˌiˈoʊ

Meaning: Being the CEO of something suggests you have become an expert at it.

For Example: "Daniel is such a CEO of design"

- **Cancel Culture**

International Phonetic Alphabet: ˈkænsəl ˈkəltʃɚ

Meaning: Cancel culture is an approach used to devalue the opinions or actions of a public person, business, or organization.

For Example: "Diddy really getting canceled on Twitter"

- **Cheugy**

Meaning: Anything out of style that is not trendy.

For Example: "Those shoes are so cheugy"

- **Camp**

International Phonetic Alphabet: ˈkæmp

Meaning: Something sarcastically stylish.

For Example: One might consider Crocs to be of the camp aesthetic.

- **Catch These Hands**

International Phonetic Alphabet: ˈkætʃ ˈðiz ˈhændz

Meaning: To start a fight. This phrase tends to be used in contentious situations.

For Example: "If Dylan continues talking shit, he is going to catch these hands"

- **Common W or L**

International Phonetic Alphabet: ˈkɑmən ˈdəbəlju ɔr ˈɛl

Meaning: To be in agreement or disagreement with something carried out or expressed implies that it is a "common W" or "common L," in which the "W" represents for a "win" and the "L" stands for a "loss."

For Example:

- **CD9**

International Phonetic Alphabet: ˌsiˈdi

Meaning: CD9 stands for Code 9

For Example: "C9, I can't pick now, my mom is homes here!"

- **Clapback**

International Phonetic Alphabet: ˈklæp ˈbæk

Meaning: A strong or clever reply to a person's criticism or attack is referred to as a clapback.

For Example: "Dave's clapback was on point, she didn't stand a chance"

- **Cringe**

International Phonetic Alphabet: ˈkɹɪndʒ

Meaning: An expression for a situation that feels extremely awkward or unpleasant.

For Example: "That guy won't stop and is so cringe!"

- **Curve**

International Phonetic Alphabet: ˈkɝv

Meaning: This is a term for disregarding or turning down a person's romantic approaches.

For Example: She totally curved him, it was so embarrassing

D

- **Dank**

International Phonetic Alphabet: ˈdæŋk

Meaning: Something that is dank is very good or high quality.

For Example: "Guy, that chain is Dank"

- **Drip**

International Phonetic Alphabet: ˈdɹɪp

Meaning: Drip is another name for swag and denotes a fashionable or appealing trend.

For Example: "I really loved her drip."

- **Drag**

International Phonetic Alphabet: ˈdɹæg

Meaning: You are making fun or shaming someone whenever you drag them. It's similar to roasting someone.

For Example: "Dele was dragged on TikTok all though the week"

- **Delulu**

International Phonetic Alphabet: dɪˈluʒənl̩

Meaning: "Delulu" is an informal term for "delusional." It can also be a way of describing a person who maintains excessively ambitious concepts or opinions.

For Example: "I think my ex wants me back, she must be dell"

- **Do Your Big One**

International Phonetic Alphabet: ˈdu jɚ ˈbɪɡ ˈwən

Meaning: This is a clever way of communicating the fact that you have been doing well on your own.

For Example: "Dave has been doing his big one, he just got promoted again"

- **Dupe**

International Phonetic Alphabet: ˈdup

Meaning: The term "dupe," which is an abbreviation for "duplicate," is often used when referring to an alternative choice, often a cheaper version of clothing or makeup.

For Example: "This bag is a dupe of Gucci's."

- **Dab**

International Phonetic Alphabet: ˈdæb

Meaning: A dancing step executed as a victory expression.

For Example: "He dabbed on all his critics."

- **Diamond Hands**

International Phonetic Alphabet: ˈdaɪmənd ˈhændz

Meaning: The expression "diamond hands" denotes the state of clinging onto a position that involves substantial financial risk.

For Example: It was dangerous, but my beau has diamond hands. She refused to give up her cryptocurrency stake till she earned back her entire $25,000.

- **DMs**

International Phonetic Alphabet: dɚˈɹɛkt ˈmɛsɪdʒ

Meaning: A form of writing for direct messages.

For Example: "I need to send Drake a DM tomorrow."

- **Don't Yuck My Yum**

International Phonetic Alphabet: ˈdoʊnt ˈjək ˈmaɪ ˈjəm

Meaning: It implies that it is inappropriate to express disdain or hatred toward something that someone else finds enjoyable.

For Example: Don't yuck is yum, if that is what he wants

E

- **Extra**

International Phonetic Alphabet: ˈɛkstɹə

Meaning: Behaving in an over-exaggerated, dramatic in nature, or extravagant style.

For Example: "His speech was so extra, he didn't need to flex on us like that"

- **Era**

International Phonetic Alphabet: ˈɛrə

Meaning: Used frequently to describe an individual's phase in life.

For Example: "She's in her baby girl era".

- **E-Boy or E-Girl**

International Phonetic Alphabet: iˈbɔɪ   ˈiˈgɝˑl

Meaning: Much like semi-emo or goth culture, e-boys and e-girls use the world of internet as an avenue for self-expression.

For Example:

F

- **Fam**

International Phonetic Alphabet: ˈfæm

Meaning: Fam is an abbreviation of family

For Example: "That's my fam man"

- **Finna**

Meaning: Finna is the abbreviation for "I'm going to."

For Example: "I'm finna get to the store later today."

- **Finesse**

International Phonetic Alphabet: fəˈnɛs

Meaning: The use of finesse is to mislead or manipulate someone or a situation so as to get what you want.

For Example: "Dale really finessed his way to that promotion"

- **Fanum Tax**

International Phonetic Alphabet: ˈtæks

Meaning: The stealing of food by friends.

For Example: "Jake fanum taxed our lunch"

- **FR**

International Phonetic Alphabet: ˈɛfˈɑr

Meaning: For real

- **Fell Off**

International Phonetic Alphabet: ˈfɛl ˈɔf

Meaning: When an individual loses their appeal or significance after experiencing popularity.

For Example: "Man, Smokes really fell off with that new release."

- **Flex**

International Phonetic Alphabet: ˈflɛks

Meaning: Flexing is a way of boasting or flaunting yourself.

For Example: "Bella is always flexing her new phone, ugh."

- **FOMO**

International Phonetic Alphabet: ˈɛfˈoʊˈɛmˈoʊ

Meaning: Acronym for Fear of missing out.

For Example: "I don't want to miss this bull run, I think I have serious FOMO."

- **Fauci Ouchie**

International Phonetic Alphabet: ˈfɔsi

Meaning: A Fauci Ouchie is a reference to the COVID-19 vaccination that celebrates Dr. Anthony Fauci, an expert in public health and vaccine advocate.

- **Fire/Trash**

International Phonetic Alphabet: ˈfaɪɚ / ˈtɹæʃ

Meaning: Fire constitutes a beautiful event, but trash is something terrible.

For Example: "The concert was fire"

- **Fit**

International Phonetic Alphabet: ˈfɪt

Meaning: Fit is the shorten form for writing outfit.

For Example: "Your birthday fit is the bomb."

- **Fleek**

International Phonetic Alphabet: ˈflik

Meaning: It's a different way of saying on point.

For Example: "He's dance moves were so on fleek, MJ will be proud."

- **Fit Check**

International Phonetic Alphabet: ˈfɪt ˈtʃɛk

Meaning: Defines the process of evaluating a person's clothing.

For Example: "Dave did a fit check for the entire squad before we headed out."

G

- **Ghosting**

International Phonetic Alphabet: goʊstɪŋ

Meaning: Ghosting someone refers to when you stop responding to someone's texts or ignore them completely without explanation.

For Example: "They ghosted me after our third meeting."

- **Guap**

Meaning: Loads and loads of money.

For Example: "Mike has got guap"

- **G.O.A.T.**

International Phonetic Alphabet: ˈdʒiˈoʊˈeɪˈti

Meaning: An acronym denoting "The Greatest of All Time." an abbreviation for an incredibly outstanding person.

For Example "MJ is the GOAT of basketball"

- **Gucci**

International Phonetic Alphabet: ˈɡutʃi

Meaning: This informal expression implies that a certain thing is okay or good.

For Example: "That's Gucci."

- **Glow-Up**

International Phonetic Alphabet: ˈɡloʊˈəp

Meaning: A "glow-up" is a facelift or transformation of some sort from terrible to good.

For Example: "Naomi has really glowed up from the last time we hung out"

- **Gaslighting**

International Phonetic Alphabet: ˈɡæsˌlaɪtɪŋ

Meaning: Leading someone to have doubts about their understanding of the truth.

For Example: "She really gaslighted him."

- **Gyat**

Meaning: Abbreviation for "God Damn". used usually when someone sees a person (which is usually a woman) with a voluptuous body or protruding buttocks.

For Example: "That girl has quite the Gyatt!"

- **Goals**

International Phonetic Alphabet: ˈɡoʊlz

Meaning: "Goals" is a word used when something sparks aspirational desire or whenever two items fit exceptionally well together.

For Example: "The Obamas are couple goals"

GRWM

International Phonetic Alphabet: ˈdʒiˈɑrˈdəbəljuˈɛm

Meaning: "Get Ready With Me" is what this implies. Influencers often share their beauty or lifestyle procedures on social media channels while they get ready for their day or for an important event.

For Example: "GRWM for the Oscars"

- **Giving**

International Phonetic Alphabet: ˈɡɪvɪŋ

Meaning: It's used to express the vibe or aura of something.

For Example: "those shoes are giving 02s."

- **Gatekeeper**

International Phonetic Alphabet: ˈɡeɪtˌkipɚ

Meaning: A gatekeeper aims to limit who can access certain opportunities and information.

For Example: "He was just gatekeeping all the job opportunities"

H

- **High-key**

International Phonetic Alphabet: ˈhaɪˈki

Meaning: Being high-key is simply the opposite to being low-key.

For Example: "I high-key need to travel very soon."

- **Hits Different**

International Phonetic Alphabet: ˈhɪts ˈdɪfɹənt

Meaning: Anything that hits differently is considerably more effective than it normally is.

For Example: "A shower in this weather will definitely hit different."

- **Hold This L/You Took An L**

International Phonetic Alphabet: ˈhoʊld ˈðɪs ˈtʊk ən ˈɛl

Meaning: Comments spoken to an individual who fell short at something.

For Example: "You really took an L with that argument"

- **Heather**

International Phonetic Alphabet: ˈhɛðɚ

Meaning: A "Heather" is regarded as a stunning, admirable individual who everybody wishes to be like.

For Example: "Dave Marley is such an Heather"

- **Hypebeast**

International Phonetic Alphabet: ˈhaɪp ˈbist

Meaning: A hypebeast is an individual who, rather than being more distinctive, is obsessed with stuff that is in trend.

For Example: "She really is an hype beast, you can't catch her wearing something basic"

I

- **Iykyk**

Meaning: This an acronym for "if you know, you know."

For Example: "They are eventually going to reduce the price, IYKYK"

- **I'm Weak**

International Phonetic Alphabet: ˈaɪm ˈwik

Meaning: This is simply a different expression you could use to convey your amusement.

For Example: "His jokes really made me weak"

- Ick

Meaning: Made use of, especially in a dating context, to express disgust.

For Example: "She really gives me the ice, I can't stand her."

- **IJBOL**

International Phonetic Alphabet: ˈaɪˈdʒeɪˈbiˈoʊˈɛl

Meaning: An acronym for the expression "I just burst out laughing"

For Example: "That was really funny, IJBOL."

- **I oop**

International Phonetic Alphabet: aɪ ˈup

Meaning: Used to communicate amusement, dread, or embarrassment.

For Example: "Did she just shit her pants? I oop."

- **It's Sending Me**

International Phonetic Alphabet: ˈɪts ˈsɛndɪŋ ˈmi

Meaning: It suggests that a particular thing is extremely amusing.

For Example: "Bruv that analogy is really sending me."

- **I'm Baby**

International Phonetic Alphabet: ˈaɪm ˈbeɪbi

Meaning: It can be used when someone feels incapable or powerless in a certain aspect of life.

For Example: "We really have to help me, I'm baby."

- **I'm Dead**

International Phonetic Alphabet: ˈaɪm ˈdɛd

Meaning: "I'm dead" is used when something is so funny it causes one to laugh to hard.

For Example: "Did you see the stunt they pulled? I'm dead man."

- **It's the "X" for Me**

International Phonetic Alphabet: ˈɪts ðə __ fɚ ˈmi

Meaning: "It's the __ for me" is a flexible expression that emphasizes a specific feature of an individual's look or actions that either appeals to them or turns them off.

For Example: "It's the haircut for me"

J

- ### JOMO

International Phonetic Alphabet: ˈdʒeɪˈoʊˈɛmˈoʊ

Meaning: JOMO is simply the acronym for Joy of missing out.

For Example: "I hearing how the event turned out, I certainly got some JOMO."

K

- ### Karen

International Phonetic Alphabet: kɚˈɹɛn

Meaning: This expression typically refers to a white woman in the middle years who tends to take exception at almost any solution provided by someone else.

For Example: "Ugh, the woman is such a Karen"

L

- ### L

International Phonetic Alphabet: ˈɛl

Meaning: The slang term "W" is opposite to "L." In place of using "W" to signify a victory, you use L as a reference to a defeat.

For Example: "The game was well played but we still took an L."

- **Let Him Cook**

International Phonetic Alphabet: ˈlɛt ˈhɪm ˈkʊk

Meaning: Encourage one to go on unrestrained with the expectation that the end result might turn out at least moderately amusing.

For Example: "Chill, let him cook."

- **Lewk**

Meaning: Anything that is distinctively associated with your signature style is referred to as a lewk.

For Example: "I don't really fancy jewleries, but it seems to be her lewk."

- **Lit**

International Phonetic Alphabet: ˈlɪt

Meaning: Is an expression that can be used to describe someone who is high or in a vibrant exciting setting.

For Example: "The after part really got me lit."

- **Lives Rent-Free**

International Phonetic Alphabet: ˈlɪvz ˈɹɛntˈfɹi

Meaning: If you catch yourself thinking about or worrying about a person or thing, regardless of whether you're aware that they aren't thinking about you, it means that they or that thing "live rent-free" in your head.

For Example: "James has been living rent free in my head since that altercation"

- **Low-Key**

International Phonetic Alphabet: ˈloʊˈki

Meaning: Used as a means of expressing an urge or feeling without becoming excessively dramatic.

For Example: "They're trying to keep the gender reveal loweky."

- **LMIRL**

International Phonetic Alphabet: ˈɛlˈɛmˈaɪˈɑrˈɛl

Meaning: Let's Meet In Real Life is the literal meaning of this acronym, which is frequently utilized in texts.

For Example: "Are you available next month? LMIRL"

- **Lituation**

International Phonetic Alphabet:

Meaning: This is a combination of the words situation and lit which refers to a situation really exciting.

For Example: "This birthday is a lituation!"

- **Lame**

International Phonetic Alphabet: ˈleɪm

Meaning: Uncool, boring.

For Example: "This conference is really lame, there was totally no need for it."

M

- **Mood**

International Phonetic Alphabet: ˈmud

Meaning: Mood is a way to communicate how you're feeling or to identify to or agree with something.

For Example: "Mood, dead."

- **Menty B**

Meaning: Monty b is a another way of communicating that someone is experiencing a mental breakdown.

For Example: "I had a meaty b all through last month."

- **Mid**

International Phonetic Alphabet: ˈmɪd

Meaning: The expression "mid" is an informal abbreviation for "middle," suggesting something regarded as merely acceptable, inadequate or mediocre.

For Example: "The new Blood and Water Series is just mid."

- **Mittens**

International Phonetic Alphabet: ˈmɪtn̩z

Meaning: It's an expression used to refer to an event that wasn't exceptionally outstanding yet was not terrible.

For Example: "I just saw our finals result, it was mittens."

- **Moots**

International Phonetic Alphabet: ˈmuts

Meaning: Mutuals—sometimes written as moots—are couples of individuals who interact and follow each other on social networking.

For Example: "Dave and I are moots on Tiktok"

- **Main-Character Syndrome**

International Phonetic Alphabet: ˈmeɪnˈkɛrɪktɚ ˈsɪnˌdɹoʊm

Meaning: Being a self-absorbed or self-indulgent personality defines what entails to act like a "main character".

For Example "She won't stop bittering about scene, she acts like she's the main character."

N

- **NPC**

International Phonetic Alphabet: ˈɛnˈpiˈsi

Meaning: Indicates a "non-playable character," an expression that describes a person who cannot think on their own.

For Example: "I don't like how he acts like a NPC, it irks me out"

- **Not you**

International Phonetic Alphabet: ˈnɑt ˈju

Meaning: To make fun of someone.

- **No Cap**

International Phonetic Alphabet: ˈnoʊ ˈkæp

Meaning: Saying "no cap" implies honesty. The phrase is additionally appropriate in reference to a person who appears to be sincere or keeping it real.

For Example: "No cap, I believe you man."

O

- **Oof**

Meaning: This could be used as a means of expressing unease, tension, or despair.

- **OOTD**

International Phonetic Alphabet: ˈoʊˈoʊˈtiˈdi

Meaning: This is an acronym for "Outfit Of The Day".

For Example: "Beyonce's OOTD was on sleek."

- **Opp**

International Phonetic Alphabet: ˈɑp

Meaning: An opponent, also referred to as an opp, is a rival or adversary who seeks to harm you in some manner.

For Example: "The Bulls new obviously our Opp in this tournament"

- **Out of Pocket**

International Phonetic Alphabet: aʊt əv ˈpɑkət

Meaning: An individual acting improperly or making unpleasant or abusive remarks is said to be acting out of pocket.

For Example: "Did you listen to his address to congress? That was really out of pocket for him."

- **OK Boomer**

International Phonetic Alphabet: oˈkeɪ ˈbumɚ

Meaning: The expression "OK boomer" is used as a clapback whenever individuals from older generations post offensive or condescending remarks about members of the younger demographic on the internet. It's also used sarcastically or ironically to brush off out-of-touch comments made by people of all ages.

For Example: "Ok boomer, if that's what you have to say."

P

- **Periodt**

Meaning: A humorous intentional spelling of "period." Periodt are used to signal the ending of a comment or the conclusion of an argument.

For Example: "I will out last her in a competition any day any time and that's on periodt."

- **Pick Me**

International Phonetic Alphabet: ˈpɪk ˈmi

Meaning: A girl who tries to present herself as "not like other girls" to attract the attention of boys is referred to as a Pick Me Girl, or somebody having Pick Me vibe.

For Example: "She's such a pick me, ugh"

- **POS**

International Phonetic Alphabet: ˈpɑs

Meaning: "POS" is an abbreviation that refers to Parents Over Shoulder in texting or chatting.

For Example: "Don't send that yet, POS"

- **Pluh**

Meaning: Used as a means of ending a conversation whenever there is nothing more to be said.

R

- **Rizz**

Meaning: A shortened form of "charisma" Appearing charming, flirty, and exhibiting slick moves especially when it has to do with romanticizing someone defines what is considered to have rizz.

For Example: "You don't even have any razz, that's why you are single."

- **Ratio**

International Phonetic Alphabet: ˈɹeɪʃiˌoʊ

Meaning: When someone's reply generates more likes and positive feedback than the original post it is responding to, particularly on Twitter or TikTok.

For Example: "Take this ratio."

S

- **Stan**

International Phonetic Alphabet: ˈstæn

Meaning: The expression combines the two words "stalker" and "fan." Becoming a stan for someone is a sort of non-creepy obsession.

For Example: "I stan Michael Jordan, he can do no wrong in my eyes."

- **Salty**

International Phonetic Alphabet: ˈsɔlti

Meaning: Being resentful or upset concerning something.

For Example: "You don't have to be salty about her reaction, she is a Karen."

- **Simp**

International Phonetic Alphabet: ˈsɪmp

Meaning: An individual who goes the extra mile for the individual who they are romantically interested in or have an unhealthy crush for.

For Example: "Alaide was just simping all evening, it was embracing to see"

- **Snack**

International Phonetic Alphabet: ˈsnæk

Meaning: Someone you consider attractive is a snack.

For Example: "Datum girl, you're such a snack"

- **Sip Tea**

International Phonetic Alphabet: ˈsɪp ˈti

Meaning: As a counterpart to "spilling the tea," sipping tea implies taking in rumors as opposed to talking about them.

For Example: "Belair and I were just sipping tea last night, it was really interesting."

- **Sheesh**

International Phonetic Alphabet: ˈʃiʃ

Meaning: Sheesh is a way of praising someone whenever they look beautiful or perform well.

For Example: "Sheesh, that performance was the bomb, congratulations man"

- **Sis**

International Phonetic Alphabet: ˈsɪs

Meaning: This expression, which is a shorter form of "sister," is usually used for greeting friends most especially between ladies.

For Example: "Hey sis, are you ready to go?"

- **Sus/sussy**

International Phonetic Alphabet: ˈsəs

Meaning: Sus is short for "suspicious," and generally refers to anything fishy or strange.

For Example: "Guy, you've been acting suspicious all day, what's your deal?."

- **Snatched**

International Phonetic Alphabet: ˈsnætʃt

Meaning: When someone is hot, and looks amazing, particularly in their attire they are said to be snatched.

For Example: "Hey babes, you look so snatched in that fit."

- **Smol**

Meaning: Something very small, and most of the time it's quite charming.

For Example: "That dog is so smol"

- **Say Less**

International Phonetic Alphabet: ˈseɪ ˈlɛs

Meaning: You understand it, and no need to further elaborate.

For Example: "Say less, I've got this"

- **Slay**

International Phonetic Alphabet: ˈsleɪ

Meaning: To deliver or look especially good.

For Example: "You really played that runaway, weldone babe."

- **Situationship**

Meaning: A relationship can be classified as a situationship if it involves more than friendship yet not quite a couple.

For Example: "I can't continue with this suituationship, we need to define what we are doing."

- **Skrrt**

Meaning: Skrrt is an Example of a remark which is intended to sound like tyres that are screeching.

- **Squad**

International Phonetic Alphabet: ˈskwɑd

Meaning: A social circle consisting up of friends.

For Example: "I've got the best squad in the world"

- **Shade**

International Phonetic Alphabet: ˈʃeɪd

Meaning: To discreetly degrade or criticize someone.

For Example: "Did Nick Minaj just shade Shaffy?."

- **Savage**

International Phonetic Alphabet: ˈsævɪdʒ

Meaning: Used to define someone who can be utterly or ruthlessly truthful or blunt

For Example: "That was such a savage response from her."

- **Shook**

International Phonetic Alphabet: ˈʃʊk

Meaning: Encountering surprise or shock. because the event you're experiencing defies comprehension.

For Example: "I can't believe I got the new Jordans for that price, I'm shook"

- **Side Eye**

International Phonetic Alphabet: ˈsaɪd ˈaɪ

Meaning: Throwing someone a "side eye" is a disapproving glance at a statement they made or a decision they took.

For Example: "I don't know why she was just giving Taylor Swift the side eye throughout the event."

- **Slap**

International Phonetic Alphabet: ˈslæp

Meaning: "Slap" is a term that describes wonderful things, for instance, incredible music or food that tastes good.

For Example: "That cocktail really slaps."

- **Sleep On**

International Phonetic Alphabet: ˈslip ˈɔn

Meaning: To sleep on something is to disregard its value or importance.

For Example: "I really slept on those offers, I should have grabbed them early on."

- **Spill the Tea**

International Phonetic Alphabet: ˈspɪl ðə ˈti

Meaning: Spilling the tea means to share the latest gossip or gist in town.

For Example: "Sis, you have to spill the tea, what happened after I left?"

- **Steez**

Meaning: Someone is considered to exhibit "steez" if their demeanor is carefreely stylish. A genuine compliment.

For Example: "I really like his steez."

- **Straight Fire**

International Phonetic Alphabet: ˈstɹeɪt ˈfaɪɚ

Meaning: Straight fire simply means that something is better than all the rest, it could also mean hot in a positive type of way.

For Example: "That kicks is straight fire."

- **Swerve**

International Phonetic Alphabet: ˈswɝv

Meaning: To "swerve" is to stay clear of a person or thing, or to avoid them completely.

For Example: "I think you should swerve Dave for now"

T

- **TFW**

International Phonetic Alphabet: ˈtiˈɛfˈdəbəlju

Meaning: TFW is an acronym for "that feeling when."

For Example: "TFW when you don't have to go to the office on Monday."

- **Take Several Seats**

International Phonetic Alphabet: ˈteɪk ˈsɛvɚ-ɹəl ˈsits

Meaning: You could tell someone to take a seat if their actions are seriously annoying you.

Example: "Stop being an asshole and take several seats!"

- **This ain't it, chief**

International Phonetic Alphabet: ˈðɪs ˈeɪnt ˈɪt ˈtʃif

Meaning: An alternative way of expressing disapproval.

For Example: "This ain't it chief, you're better than that"

- **Tea**

International Phonetic Alphabet: ˈti

Meaning: To gossip, a rumour

For Example: Bella was just spilling all the tea last night on call"

- **Thirsty**

International Phonetic Alphabet: ˈθɝ-sti

Meaning: Yearning to be liked and to receive attention.

For Example: "She's so thirsty for followers."

- **TBT**

International Phonetic Alphabet: ˈtiˈbiˈti

Meaning: An acronym for Throwback Thursday, used when sharing dated pictures or videos across social media.

For Example: "TBT to that last year when I visited Morroco."

- **To Serve**

International Phonetic Alphabet: tə ˈsɝv

Meaning: Being able to appear good is what it means by "to serve," or to serve a look.

For Example: "She was really serving on the red carpet yesternight."

- **The Brain Isn't Braining**

International Phonetic Alphabet: ðə ˈbɹeɪn ˈɪznt ˈbɹeɪnɪŋ

Meaning: Brain isn't braining is used when something doesn't appear to be comprehensible or makes no logical sense

For Example: "I can't even comprehend what you are saying, my brain is not braining."

- **TBH**

International Phonetic Alphabet: ˈtiˈbiˈeɪtʃ

Meaning: Acronym for to be honest.

For Example: "TBH I really wasn't digging his vibe."

- **Turnt**

Meaning: The term, which is just short for "turned up," is sometimes used to refer to being highly ecstatic, wild, or under the effect of drugs or alcohol.

For Example: "The guys were really turnt last night, it was wild at Smoke's"

- **Touch Grass**

International Phonetic Alphabet: ˈtətʃ ˈgɹæs

Meaning: It is aimed at individuals who seem to devote an excessive amount of their time online and might benefit by spending time outdoors in real life.

For Example: "He really needs to touch grass, his takes are starting to sound absurd"

U

- **Understood the Assignment**

International Phonetic Alphabet: ˌəndɚˈstʊd ði əˈsaɪnmənt

Meaning: This informal expression implies an individual performed a task successfully or flawlessly.

For Example: "They really understood the assignment with that dance routine"

V

- **Vibe**

International Phonetic Alphabet: ˈvaɪb

Meaning: An individual or situation's general mood, ambiance, or aesthetic can be referred to as their vibe.

For Example: "The vibe in this room is dull"

- **Vibe Check**

International Phonetic Alphabet: ˈvaɪb ˈtʃɛk

Meaning: Usually, a "vibe check" is carried out to evaluate an individual or group's general aura. "Passing the vibe check" is an endorsement for a person who gives off a sense that they're kind or relaxed.

For Example: "The exchange students really passed the vibe check in class today."

- **Valid**

International Phonetic Alphabet: ˈvæləd

Meaning: Seen to be acceptable in society.

For Example: "That option is certainly valid, we should proceed with ith."

W

- **W**

International Phonetic Alphabet: ˈdəbəlju

Meaning: W simply means "a win."

For Example: "His predictions came through, that's a huge W for him."

- **Woke**

International Phonetic Alphabet: ˈwoʊk

Meaning: Being knowledgeable regarding contemporary political and social issues.

For Example: "Jasmine is so woke, I never expected that from her"

- **Whip**

International Phonetic Alphabet: wɪp

Meaning: Whip is different word for a car.

For Example: "James cupped a new whip last year"

- **Wig**

International Phonetic Alphabet: ˈwɪg

Meaning: When anything delights you to the extent that you're afraid your wig could come off, you can say the word "wig" to express your appreciation.

For Example: "He really shook the wig off my head"

- **WYA**

International Phonetic Alphabet: ˈdəbəljuˈwaɪˈeɪ

Meaning: An acronym frequently used in text messaging that means "Where you at?"

For Example: "WYA, the game is about to start"

Y

- **Yap**

International Phonetic Alphabet: ˈjæp

Meaning: To speak unnecessarily; To use plenty of words with no any real importance

For Example: "Why are you always yapping about something you know nothing about?."

- **YOLO**

International Phonetic Alphabet: ˈjoʊˌloʊ

Meaning: An acronym for "You only live once."

For Example: "I've got to travel next week man, YOLO"

- **Yeet**

Meaning: To throw something using force that you consider is less worthy, unimportant, or simply plain garbage.

For Example: "He just grabbed my MacBook and yeeted it off the deck."

- **Yassify**

International Phonetic Alphabet:

Meaning: To "yassify" a person or thing is to get caught up in glamour to an extent that it's almost unrecognizable.

For Example: "She really yassified Beyonce with that picture she shared."

Z

- **Zombied**

International Phonetic Alphabet: ˈzɑmbid

Meaning: Used to describe a scenario where an individual ghosts someone but comes back some months later, usually used in a dating context.

For Example: "What was his explanation for zooming you?"

- **Zaddy**

Meaning: Zaddy is an expression used to illustrate and older attractive man who is well composed with an incredible style and has alot of money.

For Example: "I need to get myself a daddy, I'm tired of all these small boys"

- **Zillennials**

Meaning: Zillennials (or Zennials) are the group of people given birth to right on the cusp of the millennial and Generation Z generational usually the year 1997.

For Example: "He has to be a Zillennaials with the way he acts"

- **Zoomer**

International Phonetic Alphabet: ˈzuməʴ

Meaning: Zoomers are the generation of individuals given birth to after the millennials aka Generation Y.

For Example: "This Zoomers are really unhinged."

- **Zesty**

International Phonetic Alphabet: ˈzɛsti

Meaning: A male who acts flamboyantly or effeminately gay.

For Example: "He was just moving around zesty all evening."

- **Zooted**

International Phonetic Alphabet: ˈzutəd

Meaning: A feeling someone gets when they become high intoxicated, usually from an excessive use of hard drugs.

For Example: "I was zooted last week"

Emojis & their Meanings

Emojis are smiley faces, graphic symbols, pictograms, or ideograms that can be incorporated within text and show up on websites and in messaging applications. These are often found across a wide range of categories, like everyday items, places, weather conditions, and wildlife expressions. More individuals than at any point ever make use of emojis in their daily lives. There are well over a thousand emojis, and every single one has its own distinctive meaning. The literal meaning of emojis might appear a bit ambiguous.

Preceding Emoji

The emoticon, a more ancient type of graphic language, gave life to the trendy emoji. Emoji was not created overnight. These are simply small graphics generated by combining several keyboard characters and punctuation characters that were readily accessible.

The original version of the emoticon is attributed to American computer scientist and Carnegie Mellon University's professor emeritus Scott Fahlman:

•:-) when making a joke.

• :-(to denote gravity.

The idea itself was initially put forth by Fahlman on a Carnegie Mellon discussion board, in an entry published on the 19th of September 1982. This proves that graphic languages were being used by individuals who used computers way before the use of emojis became popular on iPhones and other smartphones.

All through the 1990s, emoticons remained widely used across discussion boards, chat rooms online, and other digital forums. The whimsical and lighthearted nature of the emoticons functioned effectively when used in these less formal scenarios. Some emoticons evolved to quite a sophisticated stage, incorporating various characters to generate complex visuals. The "shrugging man" is one of the most widely recognized examples of this: ¯_(ツ)_/¯

Because of the ease of use, a lot of individuals still make use of the most basic emoticons in present-day communication, but in general, individuals have begun leaning toward more dynamic emojis. Relative to their more recent counterparts, emoticons are not as appealing and communicative given that they are monochromatic and without visual detail.

History of Emoji

Japanese designer Shigetaka Kurita is recognized for inventing a few of the very first emoji, having created a collection of 12-by-12 pixel drawings in 1999. They were put together specifically for use on NTT Docomo, the most prominent cellular operator in Japan, including the i-mode mobile internet service. Having 176 unique visuals, the very first collection of emojis was mainly made up of fictional icons as opposed to real human characters. Presently being exhibited at the Museum of Modern Art in the city of New York is this collection.

The Japanese phrases for "picture" and "letter" have been merged together to create what is known as emoji, which refers to the use of emoji as a new visual language. Emojis were initially developed to be used via an emoji keyboard that would function while writing a message on mobile phones and tablets. Since it can be difficult to identify tone while reading a text message, emojis are often used to add extra meaning or emotion or to convey information in a simpler manner.

Other Japanese providers decided to make their versions of emoji shortly after NTT Docomo introduced this collection. This quickly rose to global popularity, and American companies including Apple, Microsoft, and Google sought to be part of the action. Google submitted a request for approval to the Unicode Consortium to have the emoji adopted worldwide, allowing them to become standard across all operating systems. In the year 2009, two engineers from Apple pursued the request further, then in 2010, the Unicode Consortium approved the proposal.

There were a total of 625 emoji included in the revised proposal, considerably more than what was included in the first set of 176. If the user did not have any of the original Japanese emoji keyboards set up users had to manually copy and paste the emoji from other places on the internet at first, but quickly things evolved. With the introduction of its native emoji keyboard for iOS in 2011, Apple significantly popularized the usage of emojis; Android followed shortly thereafter in 2013.

On an annual basis since then, more emoji have been granted permission by the Unicode Consortium. Artists have to submit an official request explaining the justification behind the emoji's introduction as well as its proposed design to the consortium for it to be authorized. All of these suggestions are reviewed by a group of experts at regular meetings, and the ones that are accepted are subsequently made public.

Anyone is allowed to submit design suggestions, nevertheless in 2015, the Unicode Consortium broadened its emoji selections in response to complaints that some voices had been getting greater consideration than others. The latest version of the emoji included couples of the same gender, several skin tones for each of the person-based emoji, and male and female characters for every professional emoji, as opposed to only men. Since that time, the consortium has grown the representation of individuals who are disabled and added a gender-neutral avatar variant.

In recent years, multiple businesses—like Apple with Animoji—have developed three-dimensional visuals and filters leveraging emoji. Other examples, including Memoji and Bitmoji, focus on generating emojis from user-generated pictures to offer a more personalized experience.

The Evolution of Emoji

1999 witnessed the introduction of emoji! Symbols for time, the weather, automobile traffic, and technology were all included as part of the initially released set.

In 2010, Unicode officially accepted emoji, introducing dozens of additional ones, notably cat expressions that symbolize weeping, fury, and happiness.

In 2015, Emoji underwent a diversity upgrade which included a pair of same-sex couples with five different skin tones.

The weightlifting woman emoji, the pride flag, and the single dad emoji became available in 2016 releases.

2017 saw the suggestions for new emojis included symbols like a mosquito that represent sicknesses like Ebola and malaria, that are intended to convey information across boundaries of language and culture.

Where Do Emojis Gain Their Greatest Usage?

Emojis can be accessed easily on any mobile device using the keyboard. Users may thereby send emojis on any page on the internet or electronic messaging that they can visit through their phone. Emojis are frequently employed in online communities, email, SMS messaging, and iMessage.

Emojis have become accessible across an extensive list of instant messaging apps utilized in offices, like Microsoft Teams and Slack. Emoji increases the possibilities for electronic communication by enabling individuals to include them as part of their messages or share them as a "reaction" to the messages of others.

Emojis have become common in business communications to communicate with customers in their native tongue, especially when posted on social media platforms. Organizations can show that they are up to date with current trends and that they have an excellent comprehension of the demographic they are targeting through the use of emojis. Some emojis may also be employed in advertising campaigns and social justice movements to effectively convey a message or show support for a cause.

The Communicative Significance of Emojis

Emojis are symbols in language that reflect emotional moods; positive communication is the setting in which these symbols are most frequently used. Emoji, according to several scholars, can be used for visual rhetoric. Emojis are symbols that can be utilized to influence communications with a sense of emotion. Emojis usually serve as a supplemental language that provides meaning to written material as opposed to bearing a meaning of their own. Emojis are symbols that can give writing greater weight and simplicity.

The Cultural Impact

Dubbed U+1F602 😂 FACE WITH TEARS OF JOY by the editors of the Oxford Dictionaries was the Word for the Year in 2015. Oxford recognized the impact of "emoji" on the culture at large and noted that the expression had grown considerably more common in the year 2015.

"Traditional alphabet scripts have been struggling to meet the rapid-fire, visually focused demands of 21st century communication," remarked Caspar Grathwohl, President of Oxford Dictionaries.

It's not that surprising that emoji, a visual script that effortlessly combines mood with versatility, is taking up those spaces. As reported by SwiftKey, the "Face with Tears of Joy" emoji holds the most worldwide usage. In its Word of the Year voting, the American Dialect Society nominated U+1F346 AUBERGINE to be the "Most Notable Emoji" of 2015.

A research study of emoji emotion was released in December 2015, coupled with the Emoji emotion Ranking 1.0. An emoji-themed opera made its Los Angeles premiere in 2016. The animated computer during the summer of 2017, The Emoji Movie made its debut.

Emojis for Happiness and Good Vibes

The emojis below portray feelings of joy and light moments by exuding happiness and excitement. These expressions, that include everything from bright smiles to affectionate gestures, convey excitement to each interaction or dialogue.

- **Emoji:**

Emoji Name: Grinning

Other Names: Smiling face

Meaning: Expresses immense happiness or excitement

- **Emoji:**

Emoji Name: Smiley

Other Names: With big eyes and a face with a grin

Meaning: Projects satisfaction with positive sentiments

- **Emoji:**

Emoji Name: Smile

Other Names: Happy face, pleasing face, face that smiles with eyes that sparkle

Meaning: An abundance of laughter and excitement

- **Emoji:**

Emoji Name: Grin

Other Names: Sweet face, gleaming with delighted eyes

Meaning: Symbolizes laughter, glee, and mischievousness

- **Emoji:**

Emoji Name: Laughing

Other Names: Squinting face emoji with a grin

Meaning: Portrays mischievous laughter

- **Emoji:**

Emoji Name: Laughing and rolling around on the floor

Other Names: Involuntarily happy and laughing

Meaning: Titled laughter

- **Emoji:**

Emoji Name: Sweat smile

Other Names: The emoji for relaxation and a sweaty, grinning face: phew

Meaning: Laughing awkwardly or discreetly finding something amusing

- **Emoji:**

Emoji Name: Joy

Other Names: Emoji of a smiley face crying

Meaning: depicts joyful tears and profound delight

- **Emoji:**

Emoji Name: A slight happy look

Other Names: Ironic grin having pain disguised within it

Meaning: symbolizes joy, optimism, or humor

- **Emoji:**

Emoji Name: Blush

Other Names: Beaming, reddish face

Meaning: reflects an immense amount of joy and optimism

- **Emoji:**

Emoji Name: Innocent

Other Names: Angel

Meaning: depicts pure and heavenly characteristics.

- **Emoji:**

Emoji Name: Heart eyes

Other Names: Heart face

Meaning: reflects affection or excitement for something

- **Emoji:**

Emoji Name: Kissing heart

Other Names: Blowing kiss

Meaning: Offers a hug as a goodbye or farewell

- **Emoji:**

Emoji Name: Kissing with eyes closed

Other Names: Kissy, kiss

Meaning: expresses admiration and devotion

- **Emoji:**

Emoji Name: Kissing with smiling eyes

Other Names: Kissy

Meaning: expresses feelings of affection in a playful manner

- **Emoji:**

Emoji Name: Yum

Other Names: mouthwatering and yummy

Meaning: Denotes gratitude for deliciousness

- **Emoji:**

Emoji Name: Tongue Stuck out

Other Names: Tongue out

Meaning: communicates joy, excitement, and charm

- **Emoji:**

Emoji Name: Tongue stuck out with a winking eye

Other Names: Crazy

Meaning: used to engage in humorous conversation

- **Emoji:**

Emoji Name: Crazy face

Other Names: Goofy face

Meaning: Exhibits enthusiasm or silliness

- **Emoji:**

Emoji Name: Hugging face

Other Names: Hugging

Meaning: expresses affection towards a person

- **Emoji:**

Emoji Name: Partying face

Other Names: Let's party!

Meaning: communicates feelings of happiness and excitement

Emojis for Disorientation and Disarray

Lack of Understanding and Perplexity Emojis depict various kinds of confused or unclear feelings. Emojis such as these can be used in a wide range of scenarios to communicate confusion, reluctance, or uncertainty. These give online interaction an additional dimension by aiding in expressing the feelings of times of uncertainty concerning decisions, scenarios, or beliefs.

- **Emoji:**

Emoji Name: Raised eyebrow

Other Names: Quizzical face

Meaning: Displays curiosity or anxiety

- **Emoji:**

Emoji Name: Neutral face

Other Names: Straight face emoji

Meaning: communicates confusion or anxiety

- **Emoji:**

Emoji Name: Expressionless

Other Names: Straight mouth

Meaning: conveys irritation or powerlessness

- **Emoji:**

Emoji Name: Thinking face

Other Names: Thinker

Meaning: Exhibits thoughtfulness or meditation

- **Emoji:**

Emoji Name: Face with Monocle

Other Names: Detective mode put into effect, something appears strange

Meaning: implies an in-depth examination or fascination

- **Emoji:**

Emoji Name: Confused face

Other Names: Confused but not surprised

Meaning: expresses uncertainty or puzzlement

- **Emoji:**

Emoji Name: Face with rolling eyes

Other Names: Eye roll

Meaning: expresses displeasure or dissatisfaction with a person

- **Emoji:**

Emoji Name: Grimacing face

Other Names: Awkward, eek, nervous

Meaning: shows uneasiness or apprehension

- **Emoji:** 🫥

Emoji Name: Lying face

Other Names: Long nose, liar, and Fake

Meaning: communicates lies or fallacies

- **Emoji:** 🤢

Emoji Name: Nauseated face

Other Names: Don't Like and unwillingness

Meaning: Declare your overall dislike or physical discomfort.

Emojis for Disappointment and Sadness

Emojis for despair and dissatisfaction precede grief or sadness. These usually express an overwhelming feeling of depression or nothingness that accompany these feelings. These feelings, that culminate in a depressive state and a desire for comfort or understanding, could have been spurred on by loss, unmet expectations, or unforeseen circumstances.

- **Emoji:** 😔

Emoji Name: Pensive face

Other Names: Sad, sad face, sorrowful

Meaning: portrays suffering and anguish

- **Emoji:** 😢

Emoji Name: Crying face

Other Names: Tearful face

Meaning: depicts melancholy, sorrow, or dissatisfaction

- **Emoji:** 😭

Emoji Name: Loudly crying face

Other Names: Tears of sadness, sobbing, and loud crying

Meaning: Expresses overwhelming sorrow or excessive happiness

- **Emoji:** 😓

Emoji Name: Sweaty downcasted face

Other Names: Hard work, dejected

Meaning: expresses sorrow, misery. or dissatisfaction

- **Emoji:** 😫

Emoji Name: Weary face

Other Names: Exhausted face

Meaning: signifies fatigue, irritation, or weariness

- **Emoji:** 😵

Emoji Name: Tired face

Other Names: Exhausted, fed up

Meaning: implies great feeling of fatigue or exhaustion

- **Emoji:** 🥺

Emoji Name: Pleading face

Other Names: Begging, glossy eyes, simp

Meaning: denotes a deep longing or an appeal for sentiments

- **Emoji:**

Emoji Name: Confounded face

Other Names: shivering face, frowned face

Meaning: communicates nuisance, despair, and unpleasant emotions

- **Emoji:**

Emoji Name: Disappointed face

Other Names: Sad, sad face

Meaning: communicates displeasure and dissatisfaction

Emojis for Dread and Disbelief

This emoji, which is often used to communicate a shocking realization or an awful encounter, represents an overwhelming feeling of surprise or terror.

- **Emoji:**

Emoji Name: Dizzy face

Other Names: Vertigo

Meaning: expresses feeling feeling dizzy, disoriented, or lost

- **Emoji:**

Emoji Name: Face screaming in fear

Other Names: Home alone, scream, shocked

Meaning: exhibits surprise both in a good and negative manner.

- **Emoji:** 😨

Emoji Name: Fearful face

Other Names: frightened and startled

Meaning: communicates nervousness or dread

- **Emoji:** 😰

Emoji Name: Sweaty and anxious face

Other Names: Worried face, fretting

Meaning: depicts feeling uneasy, trepidation, or strain

- **Emoji:** 😢

Emoji Name: Crying face

Other Names: Tearful face

Meaning: portrays melancholy, sorrow, or dissatisfaction

- **Emoji:** 😥

Emoji Name: Sad but relieved face

Other Names: Eyebrow sweat

Meaning: reflects a mixture of comfort and despair

- **Emoji:** 😭

Emoji Name: Loudly crying face

Other Names: Sobbing, sad tears, crying out loud

Meaning: Displays excruciating sorrow or uncontrollable joy

- **Emoji:** 😧

Emoji Name: Anguished face

Other Names: Pained face

Meaning: expresses despair and dissatisfaction

- **Emoji:** 😳

Emoji Name: Flushed face

Other Names: Embarrassed, blushing face, shame

Meaning: conveys guilt, amazement, or horror

Emojis Representing Love and Hearts

The Love and Heart emojis are often used to communicate a range of feelings that are associated with love, such as passionate admiration, playful flirtation, and appreciation.

- **Emoji:** 🤍

Emoji Name: Red Heart

Other Names: Love Heart, Heart Emoji

Meaning: Romance, sincere affection, and love

- **Emoji:** 💕

Emoji Name: Two Hearts

Other Names: Double Hearts

Meaning: deeper or passionate love, bonding

- **Emoji:** 😍

Emoji Name: Heart Eyes

Other Names: Heart-Shaded Face

Meaning: affection, obsession, and enchantment

- **Emoji:** 🥰

Emoji Name: Smiling Face with Hearts

Other Names: Heart having a smile, loving face

Meaning: A caring and loving connection

- **Emoji:** 😘

Emoji Name: Face Blowing a Kiss

Other Names: Eyes widening and kissing face

Meaning: Kissing with flirty affection

- **Emoji:** 💋

Emoji Name: Kiss Mark

Other Names: Print of the lip, mark from a lipstick

Meaning: gratitude, love, kissing

- **Emoji:** 💌

Emoji Name: Love Letter

Other Names: Hearty Envelope

Meaning: love message, heartfelt message

- **Emoji:**

Emoji Name: Hugging Face

Other Names: Hugger, Hug Emoji

Meaning: comfort, warm hug, support

- **Emoji:**

Emoji Name: Love-You Gesture

Other Names: I Love You Sign, ILY Hand

Meaning: "I Love You" hand sign

- **Emoji:**

Emoji Name: Rose

Other Names: Red Rose Emoji

Meaning: beauty, love, romance

- **Emoji:**

Emoji Name: Chocolate Bar

Other Names: Candy Bar, Chocolate Emoji

Meaning: indulgence, sweet gestures

Whimsical & Paranormal Emojis

- **Emoji:**

Emoji Name: Japanese ogre

Other Names: Red beast, Oni, mask face

Meaning: portrays a hideous and terrible being

- **Emoji:**

Emoji Name: Goblin

Other Names: Red disguise, wide mask for the face, angry beast

Meaning: portrays cruelty, fury, or wickedness

- **Emoji:**

Emoji Name: Ghost

Other Names: Halloween, disappear, Snapchat

Meaning: symbolizes something ethereal or ridiculous

- **Emoji:**

Emoji Name: Alien

Other Names: Outer space being

Meaning: portrays a celestial being or something different

- **Emoji:**

Emoji Name: Alien monster

Other Names: Creatures from video games, spaceship intruder

Meaning: depicts an avatar or item from a video game.

- **Emoji:**

Emoji Name: Robot face

Other Names: Droid, robot

Meaning: displays a conventional ancient robot skull

Expressions Emojis

- **Emoji:**
Emoji Name: No mouth

Other Names: Silence, empty face, and mute mouth

Meaning: communicates despair or dissatisfaction

- **Emoji:**
Emoji Name: Zipper mouth face

Other Names: Shut lips and zip it

Meaning: used for upholding commitments or secrecy

- **Emoji:**
Emoji Name: Face with thermometer

Other Names: Sick, ill

Meaning: expresses illness or discomfort

- **Emoji:**
Emoji Name: Face with head bandage

Other Names: unstable, head wrapped, aching

Meaning: indicates a headache or other form of pain.

- **Emoji:**

Emoji Name: Nauseated Face

Other Names: Yuck, puke face, nasty!

Meaning: conveys feelings of being sick or revolted

- **Emoji:**

Emoji Name: Face vomiting

Other Names: Vomit, vomit out and puke

Meaning: Depicts food poisoning or disgust

- **Emoji:**

Emoji Name: Sneezing face

Other Names: Gesundheit, sneeze

Meaning: Depicts a sneeze or having a cold

- **Emoji:**

Emoji Name: Hot face

Other Names: Overheated face, so damn hot!

Meaning: Shows great discomfort or high heat

- **Emoji:**

Emoji Name: Cold face

Other Names: Coldness, Freezing face, so damn cold!

Meaning: Explains discomfort or extreme cold

- **Emoji:**

Emoji Name: Woozy face

Other Names: Drunk face

Meaning: Depicts intoxication, dizziness, or disorientation

- **Emoji:**

Emoji Name: Exploding head

Other Names: WTH, mind blow

Meaning: Communicates amazement or extreme shock

- **Emoji:**

Emoji Name: Face with steam from nose

Other Names: Victorious, passionate, and annoyed

Meaning: expresses displeasure or dissatisfaction

- **Emoji:**

Emoji Name: Face with sign on the mouth

Other Names: shouting and cursing

Meaning: Communicates intense frustration or anger

- **Emoji:**

Emoji Name: Angry face with horns

Other Names: devil horns, devil, ultra angry

Meaning: Communicates devilishness or extreme anger

- **Emoji:** 😈

Emoji Name: Smiling face with horns

Other Names: Happy devil

Meaning: Communicates wickedness or mischievousness

- **Emoji:** 💀

Emoji Name: Skull

Other Names: Death, death skull

Meaning: Depicts death or intense emotion

- **Emoji:** 💩

Emoji Name: Pile of poo

Other Names: Smiling poop, dog dirt

Meaning: Conveys humor or silliness in an irritating manner disgusting way

- **Emoji:** 🤡

Emoji Name: Clown face

Other Names: Joker, what a joke!

Meaning: Communicates humor, playfulness or creepiness

END

Thank you for reading my book.

Daniel Ford